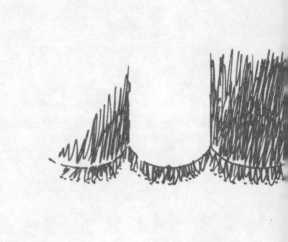

Happy, Sad, Silly, Mad

A Beginning Book About Emotions

By BARBARA SHOOK HAZEN

Pictures by ELIZABETH DAUBER
Editorial Consultant: MARY ELTING

WONDER BOOKS · NEW YORK
A Division of Grosset & Dunlap, Inc.
A National General Company

INTRODUCTION

Why do boys and girls ask questions?
Mostly because they want answers. But
sometimes they also want to wonder out
loud. A question can tell as well as ask. It
can tell about the surprising things that
grownups take for granted.

And so·this book was designed for chil-
dren and grownups to explore together.
We have called it a Beginning Book because it is an invitation to wonder and to
begin finding out. In words and pictures it
offers the youngest questioners a chance to
think—and to discover some answers for
themselves.

Library of Congress Catalog Card Number: 70-175635

ISBN: 0-448-04505-2 (Wonder Book Edition)
ISBN: 0-448-03622-3 (Library Edition)

How do you feel today?
Do you feel like smiling?
Do you feel happy?

Do you feel like making a happy noise?

Do you feel like running
and shouting, "I'm me!
And I'm glad I'm me!"
Is that the way you feel today?

Do you feel happy when someone
lets you lick the cake bowl?

Or gives you just what you wanted?

Do you feel happy
when you do something
you didn't think you could do?
Does that make you feel
like sunshine inside?

Maybe you don't feel happy.
Maybe you feel sad.
Do you feel sad
when something breaks?

Or when someone leaves you?
Does that make you feel
like crying?

Do you feel sad and sorry
when no one plays with you?

When you can't go on a picnic
because it's raining outside,
do you feel dark and gloomy inside?
Don't worry, the rain will go away.
And so will the sad way you feel.

Maybe you feel silly today.
Do you feel like giggling
and tickling someone?

Do you feel like doing something silly,
like putting all your clothes on backwards?

Or pretending you're a bug,
and saying something silly, like,
"Ug, wug. Look at me.
I'm a silly bug."

Maybe you feel like making
a silly face at someone.
Look in the mirror.
That's you!
Isn't that silly?

Mad is another way to feel.
Do you feel mad today?
Do you feel like sticking
your tongue out at someone?

Do you feel like throwing something?

Are you mad at your shoe
because it won't tie right?

Did someone do something
that made you mad?
Do you feel like hitting him
or kicking him?
Everyone feels that way sometimes.
But it's better to kick the floor.
Kicking can hurt a person.
But a floor doesn't have feelings.

Have you ever felt so mad at someone
that you wanted to shout,
"Go away! I hate you!"
That kind of mad feeling is scary.
It's like having a storm inside.
But it doesn't last long.

Have you ever felt mad
in a different way?
Have you ever felt angry at your brother
because HE got to stay up late,
but YOU had to go to bed?

Have you ever felt mad at your sister
because Grandmother said,
"Susan makes such nice letters.
I don't see why you can't do better."

Have you ever wished
the baby would go away,
because everyone always comes up
and says, "Isn't he cute!"
You don't think he's so cute.
You think he's a bother.
When you feel that way,
you are jealous.

Have you ever felt afraid?
Do you want to run
when you see a big dog
or a little bug?
Or do you want to stay
and make friends?

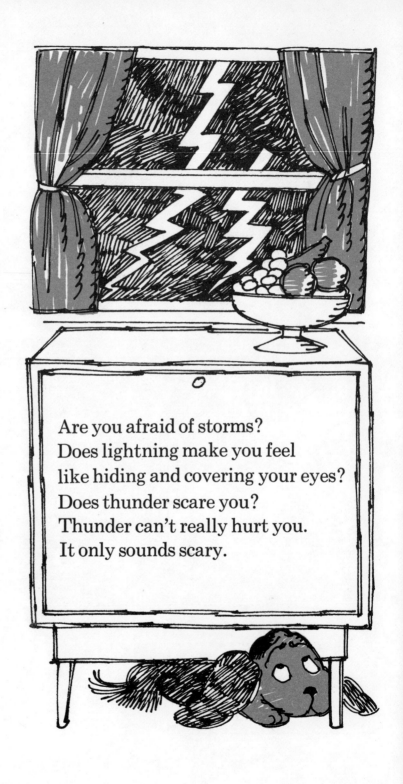

Are you afraid of storms?
Does lightning make you feel
like hiding and covering your eyes?
Does thunder scare you?
Thunder can't really hurt you.
It only sounds scary.

Maybe you are afraid of fire engines.
Maybe you are afraid of the dark.
A lot of people are—grownups, too.

Everyone is afraid of something different.
What makes you feel afraid?

Do you feel less afraid
when someone holds you close?

Have you ever felt shy?
Have you ever felt
like hiding behind the staircase
because the living room was full
of strange faces?

When someone asks you,
"How old are you?"
or "Where do you live?"
is it hard for you
to speak up?
A lot of other people
feel the same way.
They are shy, too.

Love is just about
the nicest way to feel.
Love makes you feel
like giving someone a hug
or a pat.

Love is when you want to hold hands,
even when you're not crossing the street.

Love makes you want to run to someone
and then sit on his lap.

Love is a special kind of happy feeling
that makes you warm inside.

How do you feel today?
Do you feel happy, or sad,
or silly, or mad,
or some other way?
Tell all about it.